MW01531441

Footsteps: The Poetry of Bill W. Stoner

Bill Stoner gives us an invaluable selection of poems penned from the richness of his own life experiences. His authentic wit and wisdom are rooted in having walked in the moccasins of one who brings comfort and compassion to others. You'll find just the right poem in this heartwarming treasury to illuminate the path we all walk.

—Kathryn Van Pay, Pastoral Care Counselor
Methodist Hospital, San Antonio, Texas

Footsteps: The Poetry of Bill W. Stoner helps you to think about your own journey through life, gives life's true meaning through poems with a twist that will give your own life purpose, make you see your own blessings in a new light, help you dig out of the dark hole we all face at some point in life, and make us realize we can make a difference to someone who crosses our path even though we may never know.

—Joe Neill, Businessman and Author,
Down a Bumpy Road: But Not Alone

Bill is a man God has gifted to write from his soul and spirit. You will enjoy his passion and sometimes humor in the expressions God has anointed him to pen on paper. We have personally been blessed by his gift and I believe you will be blessed also. We've had the honor of being his pastor for the last twelve years and have grown to love this faithful servant of the Lord.

—Raymond Frizzelle, Pastor
First Assembly of God, Miami, Oklahoma

As I reviewed *Footsteps: The Poetry of Bill W. Stoner*, I realized his book resembles a diary of his life because I have shared with him and Joy many of the experiences he writes about. Also as I read the book, I laughed, remembered, and cried, as Bill's deep love for his family, his life, and his farm is so evident.

—Barbara Bland Stoner,
Retired English Teacher

FOOTSTEPS

FOOTSTEPS

The Poetry of Bill W. Stoner

AuthorCentrix

Copyright © 2018 by Bill W. Stoner.

All rights reserved. No part of this publication may be reproduced, distributed, or transmitted in any form or by any means, including photocopying, recording, or other electronic or mechanical methods, without the prior written permission of the author, except in the case of brief quotations embodied in critical reviews and certain other noncommercial uses permitted by copyright law.

Printed in the United States of America
ISBN 978-1-64133-119-7 (sc)
ISBN 978-1-64133-118-0 (e)

Library of Congress Control Number: 2017954686

Non-Fiction / Poetry
18.01.08

AuthorCentrix
25220 Hancock Ave #300,
Murrieta, CA 92562

www.authorcentrix.com

To the memory of my parents, Cletis and Marie Stoner,
whose hard work and Christian values left
lasting footsteps for me to follow

Contents

Enduring Love

Bradley – God's Gift

On the Lighter Side

I believe a spoken word can have a dramatic impact on a person's life and that a written word can have an even more profound effect on a person's life.

—BWS

Foreword

Footsteps: The Poetry of Bill W. Stoner helps people get in touch with their emotions. People who read Bill's poetry have a variety of reactions, none of which are bland. Even men who like to keep a cap on emotional responses say such things as, "I really liked your poetry, but it made me cry." Others speak about being inspired, and still others say they've been touched deeply. Many talk about reading Bill's poems over and over.

For decades, Bill has been writing his heartfelt, divinely inspired poetry. In the beginning, he received messages for poems as he drove his tractor through the fields, as he performed chores, or when he woke during the night. He would jot down a note or two on a piece of paper he kept handy so he could capture the idea, then write out the poem when he was in a place and situation conducive to creating poetry.

His poetry is grounded in the teachings of the church and is informed by a long-standing Christian faith: He was brought up in the church, taught Sunday School, was a deacon for several terms, served as secretary-treasurer for many years, and used his training in drafting to design a new church that was dedicated in 1975.

I knew Bill when we were both children. We were neighbors in rural northeastern Oklahoma and rode the same school bus. After we graduated, we went our separate ways and did not see each other for decades. But in the fall of 2014, my brother and his wife died 18 days apart, and I was back in the place of my birth and formative years. I wanted to connect with my classmates and friends who had remained in the area, so I visited the ones I remembered fondly—and could find. I spent some time with my best friend in grade school and early high school, and she took me to visit her sister, Joy, and her husband, Bill Stoner.

Bill gave me a spiral-bound copy of some of his poems and knowing that I was a writer, asked me if I thought they had any merit. I was deeply moved by them and had an immediate awareness that these messages deserved wider distribution, and said so.

By divine guidance, I later stayed a few days at Bill and Joy's home, and the conviction grew stronger that these poems must be brought to light and shared with those who could benefit from them. I felt impelled to offer to help; after a time, the offer was accepted. I received direction to continue with the project—not just to type additional poems, but to prepare a manuscript for submission to the publisher. I strongly felt called to do this project, although I had other plans.

Bill's poems are so moving, so full of emotion, wisdom, and clarity that they can provide comfort during times of pain as well as guidance through confusion. And they bring a smile and outright laughter. In short, Bill Stoner's poems make lives better.

Shari Dunn
Writer/Speaker/Friend

Preface

These poems were written over the past fifty years with never a thought of their being published. I consider myself private and reserved, and keep my thoughts to myself most of the time. However, when writing poems, I reveal myself totally. I feel free to put on paper my thoughts and deepest feelings—to open my heart—which I would be extremely reluctant to verbalize.

For the most part, the poems reflect my own or family experiences, incidents, and occasions—happy, sad, and in-between. And there is a bit of humor tossed in at the end.

I feel most of the poems were divinely inspired. My prayer is that as you read these verses, they will somehow touch your spirit, uplift you, and bring you peace.

—Bill W. Stoner
Miami, Oklahoma

Faith and Inspiration

Footsteps

It was late one winter evening
    after a new-fallen snow.
I left the house and walked to a place
    where often I would go.

On a hill, just a quiet place.
A big rock in a grove of trees.
A place where I could get alone
    with God, down on my knees.

There was not a fine choir to sing,
    nor a good message from our pastor.
But I received inner strength from God,
    and that was what I was after.

While I was praying,
    darkness had settled down.
And I felt moved
    to get up and look around.

Away in the distance I saw two small figures
    walking up the hill.
I started to go toward them,
    but a small voice said, "Just be still."

As I watched, I knew it was my two sons,
    who had attempted to follow me.
But in the darkness, they had lost
    their way and could not see.

As they drew near,
I heard one say,
"Just keep walking in Daddy's footsteps.
    I know they will lead the way."

A lump came to my throat,
    and tears filled my eyes.
I wondered where in the years to come
    my footsteps would lie.

Would they lead someone
    to the streets of purest gold?
Or would someone follow them
    into the devil's fold?

Would they lead so I could point
    to them with pride?
Or would they follow a path
    that I would want to hide?

So I watched my sons taking
    giant steps in the snow.
Knowing that where my footsteps went,
    theirs were sure to go.

Someone is walking in your footsteps.
Who it is, you may never know.
But someone *is* walking in your footsteps.
Are you walking in the way they should go?

Burden Balloon Bouquet

Lord, I have so many burdens
    that I'm sending you today.
Rather than sending them one by one,
    I'm sending you a burden balloon bouquet.

As you can see,
    this bouquet is not pretty to behold.
Some of these burdens I have carried many years.
They are tattered, yet I can't seem to let go.

Some of my burdens have had a long string.
I released them, but quickly grabbed them back.
But today I committed them to you.
This time I'm on the right track.

I turned loose the strings.
I'm watching my burdens go away.
I feel light as a feather,
    and I'm walking on air.
Why did I wait until today?

Rows

Some may judge your life
    by the furrow you plow.
Do you put forth the effort
    to really learn how?

So others may follow,
    is it straight to the end?
Or looking from behind you
    is it bend after bend?

Is your furrow the same depth
    row after row?
Or is it up and down,
    like some people I know?

I thank God every day
    for my mom and dad.
For the life they lived and
    the example we had.

Their rows were always straight.
There was never a bend.
No ups and downs.
From beginning to end.

Thanks, Mom and Dad.
    Our life to you we owe.
Thank you for your example for us—
    how to pattern our rows.

Prayer of Gratitude

Lord, as I talk to you
    at this Thanksgiving time,
I would like to thank you
    for what's not really mine.

I thank you for Joy,
    my wife of forty-five years.
I thank you for always being with us,
    through good times and tears.

I thank you for James and Randy,
    our sons, fine young men.
For Sheila and Dena, their wives,
    where the grandchildren began.

I thank you for our grandchildren,
    whom I love so very much.
I know they belong to you,
    but I can love and touch.

There are Leslie and Kristy, two young ladies,
    beautiful to behold.
I know they are flesh and blood,
    but to me they are purest gold.

Thank you for allowing Bradley James
    in our lives for sixteen years.
He was such a blessing to us,
    but now I can hardly talk for the tears.

Lord, I know you have a purpose
 to use Bradley in your plan.
Although I'll never doubt it,
 perhaps some day I'll understand.

Thank you for Briana and Amanda.
They are almost grown.
Guide and protect them and
 please don't let them roam.

Thank you for Aaron,
 so loving and kind.
As a grandfather, I can say
 I'm so glad he's mine.

Thank you for Josiah and Isaiah,
 two wonderful boys,
What's on their mind now are toys,
 toys, and more toys.

Thank you for Nikki.
She has a special place.
And for little Nehemiah,
 with a smile always on his face.

Lord, thank you for Julian,
 our first great-grandchild.
Keep your hand upon him.
May he grow up meek and mild.

I thank you for my mother,
    and I thank you for my dad.
Thank you for their examples and
    that what we needed, we had.

Thank you for my brothers
    and my sister, too,
And for all of their families.
Someday may we all be with you.

Lord, I'm grateful that you
    gave your life on the cross.
I thank you that we all may be saved
    and that none will be lost.

Thank you for guiding my footsteps
    in the snow.
May they lead my family to heaven,
    where your face we can behold.

Amen.

Wedding Blessing

May God's blessing be upon you
    as you start your lives anew.
And the dreams you've had for yourself,
    may they be revised for two.

May your hopes be for the future.
Do not dwell on things past.
Set your sights on life eternal.
That's the only thing that will last.

As you go down the road of life together,
    may your path be true and straight.
And may you help carry the other's burdens
    when you see that extra weight.

May any tears be tears of happiness.
May any shouts be shouts of joy.
May any anger be toward the devil.
May any hands raised, be to praise the Lord.

May your communication always be friendly
    and your discussions never mean.
May your love for each other increase,
    and on your face always be seen.

May you cherish your time together,
    with the love of God in your heart.
When your time on Earth has ended,
    may you never, ever be apart.

Broken Beyond Repair

Our mixer wasn't working quite right.
I could see the handwriting on the wall.
With a few more days of use,
    it wouldn't be working at all.

I told my wife that with my expertise
    I would have it fixed in no time.
It would be so easy to repair
    and wouldn't cost us a dime.

The next day I took it
    to an appliance repair store.
Because after I worked on it,
    it wouldn't work at all any more.

The repair man looked a moment and said,
"Better get a new one while you're here.
This one can't be fixed.
It's broken beyond repair."

I went to the doctor to see
    if he could find
Why my right leg walked forward
    while my left one lagged behind.

After a checkup and an MRI, he said,
    "It looks as if you've had quite a tear.
You'll just have to live with it.
Seems as though it's broken beyond repair."

These situations help bring to mind
    the limitations of earthly man.
It's almost miraculous what man can do,
    but compared to God, he's like a grain of sand.

With man at the helm, we are like a ship
    lost on a troubled sea.
Broken beyond repair.
Just like you and me.

"Trust in the Lord with all your heart
    and lean not on your own understanding,"
      it's written in Proverbs three, verse five.
If we would just grasp this truth,
    we would be much more alive.

God is always there for us
    no matter what deeds we have done.
If we will call to him and ask forgiveness,
    he will forgive them each and every one.

God specializes in things thought impossible.
He went to the cross, our sins to bear.
With God, all things are possible.
To him, we are never broken beyond repair.

Good Morning, Dad

Good morning, Dad.
Another day is about to break.
It will be our first ever without you.
Oh, how our hearts ache!

We know the sun will shine again.
But now, it's so hard to find.
We can't see much for the tears.
Your leaving is still on our minds.

Dad, you were always our sun.
Your life brightened our way.
No matter how cold or dark the night
    nor how hot or bright the day.

You did not use the expression
    "Do as I say, not as I do."
You didn't talk the example. You lived it.
For that we're so grateful to you.

Your hands were not silken.
Your words were sometimes few.
But we're so proud and honored
    when we are told that we are "a lot like" you.

Stepping Stones

When adversity comes or something is said
    that wasn't heaven-sent,
Do you react as David did with Saul?
Or do something for which you must repent?

Are you going through a trial
    and you cannot find the "why"?
Each morning when you wake,
    do you feel you've lost the will to try?

Is your money gone when the month's not over
    and you still have bills to pay?
You've tried everything else.
Now it's time to pray.

If you will use these things as stepping stones,
    they will lead to a better way.
They will take you to a heavenly home,
    out of the mire and clay.

Be thankful for the adversities of life.
They are merely stepping stones.
Don't allow them to be stumbling blocks,
Just steps to lead you home.

I Asked, and I Got

I asked for knowledge.
I got to go to school.

I asked for wisdom.
I got trials.

I asked for money.
I got a job.

I asked for wealth.
I got a wife and sons.

I asked for compassion.
I got a sick calf to care for.

I asked for happiness.
I got Joy.

God will give us what we ask for.
It is our task to recognize it when it comes.

My Little Bill

What can I give Dad?
He has worked hard all his life.
To make things better for me,
    he would gladly sacrifice.

A dad who has walked miles
    up and down the rows.
Looking at the maize and
    watching the beans grow.

So I'll give him something
    to rest his tired feet.
I'll give him my horse,
    but a lot of oats he'll eat.

A nice little sorrel with four stocking feet.
I bet you'll like him. He'll be hard to beat.
Nothing dearer to me could I give away.
But I want to do this on your Father's Day.

So, Dad, as you ride him today,
May your cares be forgotten,
    as you're loping along.
Or maybe just trottin'.

So with these few words said,
    I lay down my quill.
Because today he's all yours,
    my Little Bill.

I Cried

I remember well, when I was a lad.
My brother and I, what fun we had!
Then one day I started to school.
My mother didn't want me to be a fool.

My brother was too young to go by my side.
When I got to school, I hung my head and cried.
I was older when Dad fell and broke his leg.
Mom told us, and I wondered, "Will we have to beg?"

I had forgotten that our Father in Heaven
    knew all, even right where we were living.
The neighbors pitched in and turned the tide.
I shed tears of joy. I hid my face and cried.

I was only a boy, still in my teens
    when I met the girl I wanted to fulfill my dreams.
The wedding was nearing. Soon would be the day.
"Lord, is this the girl for me?" each day I would pray.

The answer came, "Forever she will be by your side."
I shed tears of joy. I bowed my head and cried.
Our wedding day came. The twenty-fourth of August.
Joy came down the aisle, so beautiful and modest.

The ceremony started. Everyone was in place.
I looked down at Dad. He had a tear on his face.
What was I to do, as my face I tried to hide?
It was a joyous occasion. Both Dad and I cried.

About a year later, our first son was born.
It was a joyful time on that hot July morn.
Looking at him, I saw he was as perfect as could be.
I thanked the Lord for our son, who looked like me.

We were parents now. What a responsibility it brings.
We were too young; we didn't know a thing.
I thanked the Lord again for being by our side.
Emotion overtook me, and I cried.

Many years have since passed, as I sit and reminisce.
Many more ups than downs; life is not always bliss.
If I can hide these tears from your discerning eye,
    I'll go to my room and cry.

When our life is over and we reach that golden shore,
    our family will be together, forever and evermore.
No tears will be found to blur or dim my eye.
Never will you see me bow my head and cry.

Problems

-----⬆-----

The problems of life are many.
They surround us every day.
God will help us through them,
    but he won't take them away.

If we could just view problems as exercises,
    or practices, for our soul,
We could use our experiences to help others
    when, by the Holy Spirit, we are told.

It's easy to help children
    learning how to swim.
Someone once taught us how.
Now we can help teach them.

To be superb at something
    you must practice night and day.
How can we help others with their problems
    if we haven't practiced along the way?

Don't pray for fewer problems.
Don't pray for God to take them away.
Hold to God's unchanging hand.
He will guide you through them every day.

Shoveling

Is life really worth
    all the troubles you've known?

All the sickness and sadness,
    heartaches and sorrow?
And with days like today,
    you're afraid of tomorrow?

You had no hope in the past.
Even less when you look ahead.
It makes you sometimes wonder,
    "Why don't I just stay in bed?"

You feel like someone
    out shoveling snow,
With the wind blowing 50—
    and it's 20 below.

You don't know where you're going.
You can't tell where you've been.
But you must keep on shoveling.
Shovel, and shovel again.

It all seems so futile.
It won't do any good.
But look around you,
    if only you could.

Unbeknownst to you,
    out lost in the snow,
Are some of God's children,
    away from the fold.

They found the path you are shoveling,
    and are walking behind.
But you cannot see them,
    for the snow makes you blind.

So in the darkness,
    you lead them toward the fold.
In the fire they are tested
    and come out as pure gold.

Perhaps a trial to you,
    but your overcoming
May be a path to someone else
    who down life's road is stumbling.

Like the pain and the agony
    of Christ on the cross.
His overcoming
    made a path for the lost.

So never you wonder
    if life's worth the fight.
Just keep on shoveling,
    with all your might.

It not only will be certain
    that you make it in.
But because of your shovel,
    so will a friend.

Until Then, Dad

Dad, it's been a year now
    since you passed away.
We couldn't ask you to return.
But we so miss you every day.

I guess this may sound silly,
    but I've some questions I'd like to ask.
Do you see Bradley often?
And can he still run as fast?

Is his mansion close by?
Or does he live far away?
What about your mom and dad?
And is Grandpa still baling hay?

Are there cows to milk?
And does Grandma have chickens to feed?
Do you have tractors to work the ground?
Or is there even a need?

Are there mules and teams of horses?
Are there cars to drive around?
Are there places like the Grand Canyon
    and Pikes Peak?
Or is it all level ground?

How about Grandma and Grandpa Cook?
And Delma and Mom's sisters and her brothers?
And Nap and Nammy
And all the hundreds of others?

Does Jesus walk among you?
Just like common people?
Are there lots of churches?
And do they all have steeples?

Dad, it can't be long now
　　until we'll be seeing you again.
Things on earth are winding down.
I feel we're near the end.

But until then, we'll "keep on truckin"
　　even though our hearts are sad.
Until then, we'll still miss you
　　and forever will love you, Dad.

The Vision

I'm beginning to see the vision
    our pastor has seen for our town.
It's going to start in this church house,
    and we will spread it all around.

Let's get connected to the Lord
    so that we might know his plan.
Let's connect to one another
    and tell it across this land.

The Holy Ghost will fall
    like it did in days of old.
God's spirit will be moving
    and we'll feel it in our soul.

They will come from our junior high.
They will come from the high school.
They will come from the local college,
    and there will be more than a few.

They will come from north of the city.
They will come from east of town.
They will come from the south, and the west.
They will come from miles around.

Sinners will be saved.
The lame will walk again.
We feel the Rapture is nearing!
Could this be the beginning of the end?

Resurrection

To die, then live again
　　seems a stretch of one's imagination.
But if we were to look around
　　we would see it in all God's creation.

The leaves from the trees have fallen.
Their limbs look dead and bare.
It seems they never again will be green.
It all seems beyond repair.

The grass, we got our excitement
　　by sitting and watching it grow.
Might as well get rid of the mower.
Doesn't look as if we'll ever need to mow.

Tulips and daffodils.
I remember them being over there.
And now there is nothing.
The ground—it's just bare.

Birds aren't singing.
The frogs no longer be.
Flies and bugs
　　aren't around to bother me.

No baby calves in the cow herd.
No green grass for the cows, so yummy.
But they must be eating something.
They're getting bigger in the tummy.

I sense a change is coming.
A different feeling is in the air.
Springtime is arriving.
It's like a resurrection everywhere.

The trees are leafing out.
Their limbs are no longer bare.
The grass is really growing.
I can't find that mower anywhere.

Tulips and daffodils
    have burst from the ground.
Birds are singing. Frogs are croaking.
And flies are all around.

Baby calves are in the pasture.
A dozen new ones came yesterday.
And looking at the mother cows,
    several dozen more are on the way.

This all reminds me
    of Christ returning in the skies.
When the dead in Christ burst from the ground.
And we who remain shall rise.

I think it will be springtime
    when Christ returns to take us away.
Perhaps it will be on Easter.
And it's possible it could be today!

Thank You and Amen

Lord, as I come to you today,
    I ask for guidance—
    that you will show me the way.
But before I do, I would like to say,
Thank you for your goodness and
    your blessings of yesterday.

Thank you for the food I had to eat.
Thank you for the bed for my sleep.
Thank you for the clothes I have to wear.
Thank you for the assurance that you care.

Thank you for the country I live in.
Thank you for those who gave
    so I wouldn't have to give.
Thank you for giving your life on the cross,
    not only for me, but for all who are lost.

Thank you for yesterday.
Now let's talk about today.
What can I do for someone
    to brighten his or her way?

Please guide me in each step I take.
Direct me in each move I make.
I ask for wisdom to know what to say.
Please tell me for whom I should pray.

Lord, I know that in all things
    you have a plan.
Please help me to do my part.
Thank you and amen!

Plant—and Water

I can plant a seed,
    but only God can make it grow.
I can't cause the sun to shine
    but I can hoe and hoe and hoe.

I can't make the rain
    that falls from the sky.
But I can carry some water—
    before the plant is about to die.

I can't make the plant bloom
    and bring forth abundance of grain.
But I can be a reaper
    and help load it onto the train.

God only asks for what I can do
    and for me to do my very best.
If I'm faithful and do my part,
    God, for sure, will do the rest.

Stress

Stress, I believe
    is mostly created
By what we perceive.

All the everyday problems
    we have in our life.
Our interactions with others.
Our troubles and strife.

Do we view our problems
    through a magnifying glass?
When they are gone,
    do we try to make them last?

Do we make them look bigger
    than they really are?
By viewing them up close
    and viewing God from afar?

Maybe if we were to view God up close
    and our troubles from afar,
Then our problems would appear smaller
    than they really are.

Let's magnify God more
    and all our problems less.
At the end of the day
    we will have much less stress!

Quick

Be quicker to praise
    than you are to criticize.

Be quicker to lift up
    than you are to tear down.

Be quicker to find good
    than you are to find fault.

Be quicker to see the possibilities
    than you are to see the problems.

Be quicker to talk with God
    than you are about your neighbor.

Be as quick to find time for others
    as you are to find time for yourself.

Be quick to say "I'm sorry"
    should the need arise.

Be quick to say "Lord, forgive me"
    with a sincere tear in your eye.

Be quick to accept the Lord.
When you hear the trumpet sound,
You will be quick to arise,
    and will be forever heaven-bound.

Hang in There

When life's trials and troubles,
    cares, and woes
    are knocking you around
    from your head to your toes,
Hang in there!

When your money is gone
    and you've nothing to eat
    and you are worrying so much
    you can't sleep,
Hang in there!

When you can't muster
    the faith of a tiny seed
    and you feel that
    God has forgotten your need,
Hang in there!

The sun always shines
    after the darkness of night.
There's always a winner
    at the end of the fight.
Hang in there!

Trust in the Lord
    with all your heart.
Don't depend
    on your own smart.
Hang in there!

My Song

I've got a song
   springing up in my soul.
A song of praise.
Let the hallelujahs roll!

It's a song I've sung
   all my life.
Through difficult times.
Through trouble and strife.

It's a song that Satan
   tries to keep quiet.
Like a fire's dying ember
   on a cold, rainy night.

With so much water,
   it almost goes out.
But there is one little spark
   that's still burning about.

But joy comes in the morning.
The dark night is past.
And with the breath of the Lord,
   the spark is burning at last.

From a little flame
   to a roaring fire!
It helps me forget
   all the muck and mire.

And so it is
    with my song.
I'll lift my voice and
    sing all the day long.

I'll sing in the forest.
I'll sing over the plains.
I'll sing when the sun shines.
I'll sing when it rains.

I think God has given
    each of us a song.
And that we should keep singing it
    all the day long.

I can't sing your song.
    Nor can you sing mine.
But if we each sing our own,
    then all will be fine.

Family Traditions

Up before dawn.
Away to the farm.
Feed the cattle.
Go to the barn.

Work the ground.
Bale the hay.
If all goes well,
    be back at home
    by the end of the day.

It's not love of money.
It's just what we do.
One look at my bank book,
    and you'll know it's true.

Words from the Bible
    give us that drive.
They're found in Proverbs,
    chapter ten, verse five.

"A wise youth makes hay while
    the sun shines, but what a
    shame to see a lad who sleeps
    away his hour of opportunity."

Enough about work.
Let's get to the rest.
And to the parts
    that I love best.

Like Christmas dinner
    in Mom and Dad's basement.
I'm sure I can see it.
I can almost taste it.

Grace is said.
Plates are fixed.
We sit down at the table.
All thirty-six.

Following a meal fit
    for a food-loving king,
We all go to another room
    where Christmas songs we sing.

"Can we open our gifts now?"
    is what we heard.
"No. Not until we read
    from God's holy word."

Reverend Charles reads
    about Jesus's birth.
How he came from heaven
    and was born on Earth.

Then the gifts are passed out
    by the children.
The way they are piled up,
    there must be a million.

There's paper rustling and
    screams of delight.
And after it's over,
    oh, what a sight!

It's been that way since
    I don't know when.
And I truly hope
    it never will end.

.

ENDURING
LOVE

The Beginning

It was in 1953
    that I first noticed
And said,
    "This girl's for me."

I sent her some letters
    via U.S. mail.
My hopes were all high.
But to no avail.

It seemed there were others
    higher up on her list.
It would take prayer
    and determination
Before I would get that kiss.

She was sitting in math class
    when I walked by.
She looked up, and I winked
    when she caught my eye.

Like a fish on a line,
    she had taken the bait.
Now if I could just get the nerve
    to ask her for a date.

I got the nerve, and the chance,
    on a sunny fall day.
Before I could stammer out the question,
    she looked at me with a gleam
    in her eye and said, "Okay."

That was two years before
    we were married in 1958.
And it seems like every day since
    we've been on our first date.

Portrait of an Angel

I think I shall never see
    another who means so much to me.
The one who loves me all the while.
The one who always wears a smile.

The one who filled my life with joy
    when she gave me a baby boy.
The one who works the whole day long,
    while in her heart there is a song.

The one who is beautiful to behold
    and whose heart is as pure as gold.
The one who makes my life worthwhile
    just to see her charming smile.

You say an angel she must be.
That's right. She is to me.
The one I'll love throughout my life.
The one? Joy Sue, my darling wife.

Words From My Heart

If I had all the wealth
    in the whole wide world,
It would all be useless
    if you weren't my girl.

If I could put a value
    on all the girls on Earth,
They just couldn't compare
    to what you're worth.

Your pocketbook may be empty.
Your bank account may be low.
But just to know you're mine
    to have and to hold,

Means more to me than
    all the gold in the world.
Just to know
    that you're my girl.

Happy Anniversary.
I love you.

Valentine

A trip to Europe.
A frolic on the beach.
Those sorts of things
  seem out of reach.

But all it takes to make
  my grey skies turn blue,
Is to hear you say
  "I love you."

Will you be my Valentine?

Happy 23rd

---✦---

"Happy 23rd," I started to say.
But after a little thought,
I said "there's no way
    it's twenty and nine."

It seems just a short while
    since two young kids
    walked down that aisle,

With hearts full of love
    and pockets full of empty.
I didn't realize that
    times would be so scrimpy.

But with the help of the Lord
    and a lot of determination,
I've come this far
    and to the realization

That the finer things of life
    aren't silver or gold.
But children and grandchildren
    to have and to hold.

But the finest of all
    is to have a wife like you.
So Happy 29th Anniversary.
I love you, Joy Sue.

Can You Spare Some Time?

A time to go to the hill
　　and watch the sun go down.
Or maybe just spread a blanket
　　and lie there on the ground.

A time to go out and look
　　at the cattle we own.
Or maybe a quiet evening
　　without the telephone.

A time to take a ride
　　in my brand-new pickup truck.
You know it won't be long until
　　it's all muddy, and maybe stuck.

A time to look at Rocky's land
　　and consider if we should
　　get the money to buy it.
Or should we if we could?

A time to patch my jeans
　　and maybe sew on a button or two.
You know if you could do that,
　　I'd much prefer them to new.

A time to smell the roses
　　or maybe help pick up leaves.
Or just a walk in the timber
　　and admire the beauty of the trees.

A time to sit down
    to a table set for two.
Rather than in a rocking chair
    With our eyes to the TV glued.

I know you're really busy
    and bogged down to your knees.
But sometimes, one can't see
    the forest for the trees.

Your job is very important
    and I'm sure a part of God's plan.
But I don't think it was his intention
    that it all be done by one woman.

Joy, can you spare some time for me?

Jumping With Joy

Through good times and bad.
Through happiness and tears.
I've been jumping with Joy
    for, lo, these many years.

Alas, it seems our life's road
    has come to a bend.
The Joy is still here, but the jumping
    has come to an end.

I love you, Joy.
    I still want you to be mine.
And even though you're sixty now,
    you don't look a day past fifty-nine.

I Love You

I love you. I love you. I love you.
Maybe it's what you need to hear.
I know I haven't said it enough
    although we've been married 44 years.

I can put words on paper
    and sometimes make them rhyme.
But when I try to say what I mean,
    it seems I have a difficult time.

But I'm going to try to do better
    and tell you "I love you" along the way.
Even though you know it,
    I might tell you every day.

I'm so glad your dad named you Joy.
It fits you to a T.
I thank the Lord each day for you.
And I thank you
    for spending your life with me.

In the Middle

You like to sleep on forty acres.
I like to sleep on a dime.
You want to be independent.
I want you to be mine.

I like to sleep under the covers.
You like to sleep on top.
I don't like to go shopping.
You like to shop 'til you drop.

I like to go to bed at sundown.
You like to wait for the moon.
I like to get up before daylight.
You like to get up about noon.

You have a smile on your face
    that will brighten a person's day.
I have a serious look on mine
    that tends to dim their way.

You have highs and lows.
I live on a level plane.
You like it when the sun shines.
I like it when it rains.

I have fun when I work.
You have fun when you play.
I want to get things done now.
You wait for another day.

You are able to comfort
    a person along the way.
I am at a loss,
    without a word to say.

You can speak your words.
I put mine on paper.
You're like a Krispy Kreme doughnut.
I'm like a plain vanilla wafer.

My temperament runs about average.
You're either hot or cold.
I'm reserved and shy.
You are outspoken and bold.

When you go to visit,
    you think you must talk.
When I go to visit
    I sit there like a rock.

When we work together to pull a wagon,
    a good team we certainly make.
But if we pull from different directions,
    the wagon will surely break.

The Lord in His infinite wisdom
    has put variety in the kettle.
It's up to us whether fur or kisses fly,
    when we meet in the middle.

It's Coming Along

It doesn't taste like candy.
It doesn't smell like a rose.
It won't sparkle like a diamond.
But you'll be safe when the cold wind blows.

It has a sun room and a safe room.
And a three-car garage.
Joy Sue, it's really for you.
And it's not a mirage.

For forty-five years
    of giving me your life.
You are a very loving mother.
And an almost perfect wife.

A small token to give
    for what you've given me.
And I'm looking forward
    to spending forever with thee.

Happy Valentine's Day, Joy.
I love you.

House Blessing and Prayer

Lord, we thank you for this house
    at Sixteen O Seven C.
We dedicate it to you, Lord.
We freely give it back to thee.

May it be a lighthouse
    in the middle of the night.
May it be a beacon and
    shine forth your great light.

May it be a shelter
    in the time of a raging storm.
May it be a refuge
    where the cold can get warm.

May it be a house where
    only kind words are said.
May it be a house where
    hungry souls are fed.

May it be a house where
    God's love is always shown.
Let it be not only a house.
Lord, help us to make it a home.

May the sounds of grandchildren playing
    fill each and every room.
May it be a home where they are taught
    that Jesus is coming soon.

May it be a home where
    to the needy, we freely gave.
May it be a home where
    our entire family is saved.

Lord, we thank you for blessing us with this home.
Amen.

Then and Now

When we were teenagers driving down the road,
You would nearly sit on my lap.
Now that we've been married nearly 50 years,
    You sit in your bucket seat and nap.

When we were young,
    I could always reach across the seat.
It seems that you were always there.
Now when I reach for you, the console is between.
It seems that it has become a snare.

When we were first married,
    we could cuddle in our double bed.
Now I hunt to find you,
    sleeping in a king-size instead.

I think in our golden years
    we have been drawn apart.
It's not from lack of love or romantic notions.
But bucket seats, consoles, and a king-size bed
    keep the notions from our hearts.

BRADLEY –
GOD'S GIFT

Introducing Bradley

Bill has had a close and unique relationship with each of his 10 grandchildren. This section focuses on one of them.

Like the other grandchildren, Bradley spent weekends with PaPaw and MeeMaw. When Bradley was just a tyke, he was Bill's shadow; where PaPaw was, Bradley was. He insisted on dressing like PaPaw: jeans, plaid western shirt, and cowboy boots. When he was older, this attire was accompanied by a John Deere cap.

Before the era of booster seat requirements, Bradley would stand on his knees in the pickup seat by PaPaw so he could observe his surroundings, while PaPaw sang "You Are My Sunshine" to him. Bradley's response was always, "Sing it again, PaPaw."

Bradley took to the farm and ranch life the way a duck takes to water. When he was eight or so, he began to steer the tractor, and as he grew older, his expertise increased. He not only drove the tractor and combine, he mowed hay and worked on equipment. He took great pride in doing each job well; for example, it was very important to him to avoid "skips" when he mowed hay. He was efficient, dependable, self-directed, and self-reliant. All of this before he was 16!

This was a multi-faceted young man. The handsome guy with the dark hair and sparkling brown eyes was an outstanding athlete in both track and football. He was being watched by college football scouts. He had a magnetic, playful personality and was well-liked by his peers.

With Bradley's passion for the farming and ranching life, it appeared that Bill now had a family member to carry on the business he had built. Then one day the unimaginable happened: When he was 16, Bradley was killed on his way to school when a huge object fell on top of his car.

The Stoner clan was devastated, and Bill was inconsolable. Not only had he lost a beloved grandson, but so many hopes and dreams for the future were dashed that sad day in September 2000. He also had lost his likely successor.

The poems in this section express some of the emotions Bill experienced as he worked through his grief.

Why?

The cattle all walk slowly
    and somberly to eat.
It seems they know
    Bradley is not there to greet.

In the pasture a lone goose is
    standing upright and so straight.
It seems he understands.
I think he's lost his mate.

In the distance a train whistles
    its long and mournful sound.
It seems to cry to me,
    "Bradley is not around."

The seats of the tractors are empty—
    the ones that Bradley
    so eagerly would drive.
They also seem to say,
    "Bradley is not alive."

A baby calf needs a tag.
Bradley would have caught it with ease.
I finally caught it.
But now I feel wobbly in my knees.

The gates Bradley always opened
    I now will do on my own.
But I know his fingerprints are there
    as if forever embedded in stone.

The dog no longer barks.
The cats don't meow.
The horses won't nicker
The grouchy folks don't even growl!

Lord, I don't know the reason
    Bradley had to die.
But I completely trust you, Lord.
I'll try not to ask you why.

Angels on Call

I think God has a band of angels
    just waiting for his call.
When they were needed,
    they came—not one—but all.

They came with food, flowers, and prayers.
With cards and words of sympathy.
With hugs, handshakes, and phone calls.
All that means so much to me.

Until now, I knew not that they were angels.
Their familiar faces I have seen.
Like me, they had their faults.
Like some of us, a few were downright mean.

But now, they all seem perfect.
No faults can I remember.
For me they all became angels
    on that sad day in September.

Life's Game

The football game is almost over.
The Wyandotte Bears are behind.
The Bears have the ball,
    on the opponent's two-yard line.

Time is called. The coaches asked,
"Do you have any suggestions?
The defense is big! To go through that line
    is simply out of the question."

Brad said, "Let me have the ball.
    I've been given a play."
They handed off to him,
    and he ran, but the wrong way!

The fifty, the thirty, to the twenty he ran.
But in the wrong direction.
At the ten, just like in his life,
    he turned and made a correction.

Back to the thirty, then to the fifty he ran.
He dodged tacklers and hurtled over another.
The crowd was all cheering.
Everyone and their brother.

All the while his PaPaw stood quietly,
    his heart doing flips like a child.
And his MeeMaw was jumping
    on the bleachers and going wild!

The buzzer had sounded.
But Brad was still moving ahead.
The game is not over
    until the play is blown dead.

Brad made the touchdown.
He crossed the goal line.
The Wyandotte Bears had won
    thirty-two to twenty-nine.

This game is fictional.
A product of my imagination.
But the thirty-two were real.
They came forward for salvation.*

You who were hesitant,
    be quick to decide.
Ask the Lord into your heart
    where he can abide.

If Brad could tell you,
    I'm sure he would say,
"Get saved and do it fast.
The breath you're breathing now
    could be your very last."

*Bradley's funeral service was held in the gymnasium of his high school in Wyandotte, Oklahoma. At the close of the service, the officiating minister issued an altar call, and 32 people, primarily students, responded.

Ode to Bradley

Bradley,
You were the apple of my eye.
The clam in my chowder.
The light of my life.
The pecan in my pie.

The colors in my rainbow.
The star in my night.
The twinkle in my eye.
You were the future in my farmer.
The skyrocket in my sky.

You were the star in my blue heaven.
You were the sunshine in my sky.
You are the teardrops in my eyes.
It is for you that I cry.

You filled our life with happiness.
You filled our life with cheer.
How deeply we miss you
    and wish you were here.

I know you are happy there.
That you cannot return.
I guess it's just my selfishness,
    but oh, my heart does yearn.

To see your smiling face again
    and hold your hand in mine.
To walk around with you again.
It would be so divine.

I know on earth, that can't happen.
But in heaven, I hope to see you soon.
And perhaps we can farm and raise cattle.
Somewhere—maybe on the moon.

Footprints in the Sky

Bradley, it's the first of April.
    Two thousand one.
It's been just over six months now
    since your life on earth was done.

I still miss you so very much.
It's almost more than I can bear.
I see you in everything I do.
It seems that you are right there.

I know I don't know what I'm asking.
And I don't know if it's possible at all.
I don't know if it's a big task,
    or if the task is small.

I don't know if you're "confined" to "heaven"
    or if you have the universe to roam.
But by chance if you can go to the planets,
    it would mean so much to me at home,

If you could leave your tracks in the clouds,
    like your footsteps in the snow.
It would mean so much to me
    as down this road I go.

Bradley, I know my request may seem unusual.
I wouldn't want you to bend or break any rule.
But if I could see your footprints in the sky,
    as you would say, "That would be really cool!"

Forty-Four

Bradley, some time ago I wrote a poem
    about your footprints in the sky.
I haven't seen them yet,
    although every day I try.

But what I have seen,
    to me a pleasant surprise,
    is number 44.
How many times, I hadn't realized.

Last year was our 44th anniversary.
This year is your dad's 44th birthday.
I saw your mother's car with 44 on the window.
I just baled a field that had 44 bales of hay.

The road to the barn
    begins with 44.
A main road in Oklahoma
    is Interstate 44.

Going back 44 years
    plus maybe a couple more,
My basketball jersey was?
You guessed it! Another 44.

My baling tractor is a 4440.
"44" is engraved on my tractor key.
It was done before I bought it,
    but it means so much to me.

A picture of you in your "44" jersey
    sits on our shelf.
A small football sits there too
    with the number "44." What else?

I went to look at a pasture to lease.
It was several miles away.
I found it on Road 4400.
I felt your presence again that day.

Those fences really needed mending.
But the grasses were tall.
And I'm wrestling with the decision
    whether to try to lease at all.

I went to meet the owner
    to get more information.
When I left, I saw his license plate.
My, what a revelation!

It ended in 44.
Again, I felt your presence there.
It helps me with the grief,
    still almost too much to bear.

I'm going to try to lease it.
I have just come to my senses.
With 44s all around, you'll be there
    to help me mend those fences.

Who Will Sing My Song?

Who will do the mowing
when hay time rolls around?
And what about the baling?
Will the bales be just as round?

What about the swathing?
Can anyone do it as good?
I would come back and run it,
If only I could.

And what about the fescue?
Who can run that 95?
I would gladly show him how,
     if I were but alive.

The 44 on my jersey,
Who will wear it now?
Can he make those touchdown runs?
Not like I did. Holy cow!

The cut-up in the classroom,
Who will take my place?
Who will have my grin
     showing on his face?

My sisters and my brothers,
Who will tease them now?
Someone else may try,
But I really did know how!

My MeeMaw and my PaPaw,
    who will make their day?
No one can, like me.
I had my own special way.

Who will sing my song
    for my mom and my dad?
I know that when my song ended,
    it made their hearts so sad.

God gave us each a song to sing.
And we can't sing another's.
No one else can sing my song.
Not even my little brothers.

So take the song God gave you
    and sing with all your power.
You don't know when God will say,
    "This is your final hour."

Don't Weep For Me

PaPaw,
Don't weep any more for me.

You need to change those tears from sadness,
And your gloomy face to gladness.

I'm at home in heaven on high.
I'll meet you there bye and bye.

Jesus's face is so bright.
There never will be a night.

Heaven is so grand.
Almost more than I can stand.

My time on earth was great.
Now in heaven I celebrate.

I think I'll take a little stroll.
Walk down those streets of gold.

I'm so happy in Jesus's care.
Now let him your burdens bear.

I'll be waiting and watching for you.
Just be sure you make it through.

ON THE
LIGHTER SIDE

You Can Take it With You

Whoever said you can't take it with you
    didn't know my Joy Sue,
I thought, as she packed
    and gave me things to do.

There's three weeks of clothes
    for a one-week trip.
Along with some snacks,
    potato chips, and some dip.

There are bottles of water
    too heavy to tote.
Games and CDs.
No wonder I'm broke.

There are antiques and collectibles.
Prescription drugs galore.
If there's anything you need,
    she has a mini-drug store.

There is a pregnancy test.
A snake bite kit.
A telephone book.
And a sweater to knit.

There's suntan lotion.
Horse liniment for sprained ankles.
And some kind of stuff
    that will get rid of wrinkles.

There's twenties and fifties.
And a two-dollar bill.
Blank checks and credit cards.
I'm beginning to feel ill.

If I should survive
    the "fun" from this trip,
I think I shall never, ever
    get on another ship.

Practical Living?

I attended a Sunday-School class
    Christmas dinner last night.
The food we had
    was such a delight.

After the meal, the tables were moved.
The chairs were arranged around
    the Christmas packages,
    to see what could be found.

Numbers were drawn to help
    organize this confusion.
Is this a "Practical Living" class party?
Or am I having an illusion?

When your number was called,
    you could pick a gift of your choosing.
Or you could take one from someone else
    if you felt up to the bruising.

A gift could be taken only two times,
    then was declared "dead."
That sounded really strange to me.
But that's what they said.

The gifts stayed dead
    until the very end.
Then for three minutes
    they all came alive again!

When the clock started ticking,
    something came over those folks.
The packages were flying!
It's a wonder they weren't broke.

After three minutes, it stopped.
You got what you got.
That was what you ended up with
    whether you liked it or not.

The party is over.
A good time was had.
If this is "practical living,"
It's not half bad.

Hold That Thought

A songwriter, an inventor, a writer of rhymes.
All must be quick with a quill.
If they don't get it down when a thought
    comes to mind,
It's quickly gone over the hill.

Use cardboard. Scratch paper. An old paper sack.
Anything on which you can write.
If you don't catch it
    when a thought comes to you,
    it's gone, like a thief in the night.

There have been times in the night
    when I had words that rhyme
    that I thought I could hold until morning.
But when daylight came,
    they had all slipped away.
They left, without a goodbye or a warning.

A word to the wise for those who write:
Quickly put that thought down to lock it.
To do this, you must carry a pen and a pad
    and always wear a shirt with a pocket.

Change

Change works well when you're young.
But old folks don't take change so well.
If you talk about changing things to me,
    I just want to stand up and yell!

I'm not in a rut, just a routine.
My seat now conforms to my pew.
A visitor is okay—if they fit my mold.
But no more than maybe one or two.

My name is not on my space in the lot,
    but everyone knows it's mine.
And heaven forbid if someone should park there.
They just may get hit from behind.

My money I hold; my opinions I give.
As to opinions, I've got quite a lot.
And you're likely to get one or more,
    whether you like it or not.

So why make a change
    when we have done it this way so long?
We can keep singing and praising the Lord
    as long as it's the same ol' songs.

Cruise Trip Prayer

Lord, thank you for the opportunity
    for this extended fellowship.
I pray that our friendship
    can endure through all of it.

I pray for a guardian angel
    to be by our side.
To keep us from harm as we
    start out on this ride.

Guide and direct us.
Help us to have fun.
And when I get home
    may the haying be done.

Would you watch over your cattle
    just while I'm away?
I pray they don't get sick
    or stolen—or stray.

I pray for our attitudes.
That we will stay well.
That we not do anything
    that would send us to hell.

I pray for the ship.
Please keep it afloat.
Help the crew fix
    anything that's broke.

I pray for good weather.
Not too hot. Not too cold.
No tornadoes or hurricanes
    nor strong wind to blow.

That when we return we are
    refreshed and revived.
All in good health and
    all very much alive.

We'll say, "It was fun.
    Let's do it again."
But let's wait awhile—
    until our pocketbook mends.

Lord, thank you for listening.
I think I covered it all.
But I know you're always there.
If I forgot something, please call.

Do You Really Want to Know?

"How am I doing?" you ask.
Folks don't really want to know.
It's just polite to say.
Like saying "good-bye" and "hello."

"I'm fine," would be
    my usual reply.
But most likely, that would be
    a little white lie.

My aches and pains I'm feeling.
Things just aren't going my way.
I'm sure all will be fine tomorrow.
So suffice it to say, "I'm doing okay."

The Election

The votes have been counted.
Reviewed and counted again.
We still don't know who's president.
And won't 'til I don't know when.

This brings back fond memories
    that I can recall.
About my brother and I
    and a bat and a ball.

We both wanted to bat first.
How would we settle the tie?
Would it be dueling guns?
And the last one to die?

Or who could throw a rock the farthest,
    my brother or me?
Or which of us could get the closest
    to a mark on a tree?

Sometimes we drew straws
    to settle it all.
Whoever got the longest
    was to make the call.

However, on occasion,
    one of us would dig in.
And then usually say,
"It's not fair. You always win!"

And then he would say,
"Let's make it two outa three.
That would be more fair
    for you and for me."

If that didn't work,
    we would keep it alive.
"Let's do it twice more.
Let's make it three outa five."

And then we two boys,
    about ten and eleven,
    would go twice more.
Make it four outa seven.

By then we had lost interest.
And it didn't really matter
    who would be first.
Or who would be the latter.

I long for those ol' days
    when life was so simple.
Because we were totally unaware of the
    complication of the chad and the dimple.

Now with all the lawyers involved—
    standing one on top of another,
    they could reach heaven.
I bet it could be settled more fairly
    by two kids 'bout ten and eleven.

Red

I like red as a color.
A red shirt or a red truck is fine.
But when it comes to a financial statement,
    I dislike red on the bottom line.

Sometimes it is shown with a minus sign.
Sometimes it is bracketed in (parentheses).
But no matter how it is shown,
    it still seems red to me.

The solution is really quite simple.
If you practice it from beginning to end,
    your bottom line never will be red
    if you take in more than you spend.

A Few BWS Proverbs

If a silent auction
    can sell a pie,
Surely a silent prayer
    can reach the sky.

Don't think more of yourself
    than you ought.
Or your life
    may come to naught.

The higher you are
    on your pedestal,
The farther
    you have to fall.

You shouldn't be out
    when big hail is falling.
Or else your name,
    the Lord might be calling.

If you're walking on ice,
    it shouldn't be thin.
If you're going to be nice,
    you should wear a grin.

Don't go into the water
    if you don't want to get wet.
If you don't want to lose,
    then you'd better not bet.

Retirement

My friends have been asking
    why I don't slow down or retire.
I'm 75 now. Think I'll try it a day or two
    to see if it fits my desire.

I recently had surgery and need to go slow.
A good excuse not to go to the farm.
I'll retire for a couple of days.
Sure couldn't do any harm.

I'd planned to sleep in on day one,
    but I got up at a quarter to five.
I read the Bible, caught the news, and
    looked at the obits to see if I was alive.

"Glad you're here; I need some help," my wife said.
"I've written it down, on a list."
"Be glad to," I replied. "Let me look,
    and you won't need to twist my wrist."

On it was: Fold the towels, take out the trash,
    the patio needs some sweeping,
    straighten the closet, clean out the garage.
And I don't think there will be time for sleeping."

'Bout mid-afternoon, I was getting ready for a nap.
I'd been doing some serious huffing and puffing.
"Would you run to the store right now?" she said.
"I'm beginning to think you're sloughing."

On my way to the store
    I pondered the definition of slough.
If sloughing is what I did today,
    One day of retirement is enough.

Acknowledgments

I wish to express my deep appreciation to all who in any way contributed to the writing and publication of these poems.

I am profoundly grateful to my wife, Joy, for her many contributions. She typed my scribbling, which sometimes was on the back of dirty, tear-stained, paper feed sacks and at other times on who knows what. (Now I carry paper for such a need in my shirt pocket.) Joy prepared what was the forerunner of this book: She lovingly searched for and selected paper with beautiful illustrations that supported the message of each poem, then had the collection spiral bound, and I gave copies to family members and a few friends.

A sincere, from-the-heart thank you to Shari Dunn for making this book of poems a reality. She felt the need and "calling" to get it published after reading some of my poems. I had felt the poems might be beneficial to others, but I guess I was waiting on the Lord to accomplish this, and, with Shari's help, I think he has. She provided editorial consultation, prepared the manuscript, wrote the foreword, and interacted with the publisher. With her commitment, she has left her own footprint.

I thank everyone who expressed appreciation for the poems and offered encouragement throughout the years. I especially appreciate those who took time from an already full schedule to review *Footsteps*: Pastor Raymond Frizzelle, Danny Jones, Joe Neill, Barbara Bland Stoner, and Kathryn Van Pay.

Thanks to Randy, Terry, Garret, Danny, Julie, and Cheri, who kept the ranch going while I took some time off to finish *Footsteps*.

Finally, and most of all, thanks to the Lord, who inspired many of the poems and for allowing each of the above to cross my path and be a blessing to me. May these poems be a blessing to others and help see them through difficulties in this life.

CPSIA information can be obtained
at www.ICGtesting.com
Printed in the USA
FSHW011213210319
56480FS

9 781641 331197